D1373323

12 SCIENTISTS
WITH DISABILITIES

by Susan Perry

STORY LIBRARY
MORE TO EXPLORE

www.12StoryLibrary.com

12-Story Library is an imprint of Bookstaves.

Photographs ©: Paul E. Alers/NASA, cover, 1; Associated Press, 4; PD, 5; University of Michigan/YouTube, 6; University of Michigan/YouTube, 7; Paul E. Alers/NASA, 8; M.Weiss/CXC/NASA, 9; PD, 9; Joi Ito/CC2.0, 10; Ryan Lash/TED Conference/CC2.0, 11; Marla Aufmuth/TED Conference/CC2.0, 12; ROSAT/MPE/NASA, 13; PD, 13; FPG/Getty Images, 14; PD, 15; BLACKSWAN Foundation/CC2.0, 16; NIH/US National Library of Medicine/PD, 17; Eugène Pirou/PD, 17; Royal Society of Medicine: Photographic and Film Unit/PD, 17; Aldona Griskeviciene/Shutterstock.com, 17; Kathy Hutchins/Shutterstock.com, 18; tetzl/CC2.0, 19; Scott Bauer/USDA/PD, 19; PD, 20; NASA, 21; Peggy Greb/USDA/PD, 22; USDA/PD, 23; David Hall/USDA ARS/PD, 23; Xose Kakane/CC4.0, 24; Joris van den Heuvel/Shutterstock.com, 25; PD, 25; PD, 26; Leo Lesquereux/PD, 27; National Council on Disability/PD, 28; wavebreakmedia/Shutterstock.com, 29

ISBN
9781632357571 (hardcover)
9781632358660 (paperback)
9781645820413 (ebook)

Library of Congress Control Number: 2019938638

Printed in the United States of America
October 2019

About the Cover

Stephen Hawking delivering his 2008 speech, "Why We Should Go to Space," in honor of NASA's 50th anniversary.

Access free, up-to-date content on this topic plus a full digital version of this book. Scan the QR code on page 31 or use your school's login at 12StoryLibrary.com.

Table of Contents

Geerat Vermeij: Studying Fossils

Geerat Vermeij uses his sense of touch to learn how mollusks lived hundreds of millions of years ago.

Vermeij studies mollusks in a different way than other scientists. Soon after he was born in the Netherlands in 1946, doctors discovered he had a serious eye disease. It made him go blind when he was three years old. So Vermeij uses his hands—his sense of touch—rather than his eyes to learn about mollusks and their fossils.

Vermeij can discover many things when he rubs his fingers over a mollusk fossil that's hundreds of millions of years old. For example, by feeling the fossil's bumps and grooves he can tell how other creatures once attacked the mollusk with their jaws or claws.

Geerat Vermeij is one of the world's leading paleontologists. These are scientists who study fossils. He is especially famous for studying the fossils of mollusks. Mollusks are animals that have a soft body that is usually inside a hard shell. Examples of mollusks are snails, slugs, clams, and oysters.

Vermeij has lived in the United States since he was 10 years old. But his

Bumps and grooves in mollusk shells provide clues about their predators.

research has taken him around the world. To find mollusks and their fossils, he has waded into snake-filled swamps and shark-infested seas. He once put his hand into a hole on an ocean reef. He grabbed what he thought was a snail. But it was an eel. It bit him. The bite hurt, but he was okay.

Vermeij says being a paleontologist is fun. He gives this advice to kids who want to become scientists: Work hard. And if you fail at something, don't get discouraged. Just try again.

200+
Scientific papers Vermeij has written

- Vermeij writes on a Braille typewriter.
- Braille is a way of printing that uses raised dots to represent letters in the alphabet.
- People read the dots by moving their fingers across them.

Karin Muraszko: Helping Children Get Well

Karin Muraszko in 2009.

like any other child. They focused on what she could do, not what she couldn't do.

And Muraszko went on to do quite a lot. After several operations on her spine and legs, she learned to walk with a leg brace. She also did really well in school. Her favorite subject was science. She especially liked learning about how plants, animals, and other living things work.

Karin Muraszko was born in 1957 with spina bifida. It's a medical condition that causes the nerves in the spine to be damaged. Spina bifida can make it difficult to walk. It can also cause brain damage.

Doctors told Muraszko's parents that she would never be "normal." They said she should be sent away to live in an institution. But Muraszko's parents refused to send her away. They raised her in their home in New Jersey, just

Muraszko decided to become a doctor—a special type known as a neurosurgeon. That's a doctor who does surgery to fix problems in people's brains or spines. Today, Muraszko is one of the best-known neurosurgeons in the United States. Most of her patients are children. She remembers how much surgeons helped her when she was growing up. Now she does the same for other children.

3,600
Neurosurgeons in the United States

- Only 219 of those neurosurgeons are women.
- Karin Muraszko says that's too few.
- She hopes more girls will be inspired to become neurosurgeons.

LEADING THE WAY

The first woman neurosurgeon was a British doctor named Diana Beck. She became a neurosurgeon in the early 1940s. That was during World War II. After the war, one of her patients was A.A. Milne. He later wrote the children's books about Christopher Robin and Winnie-the-Pooh.

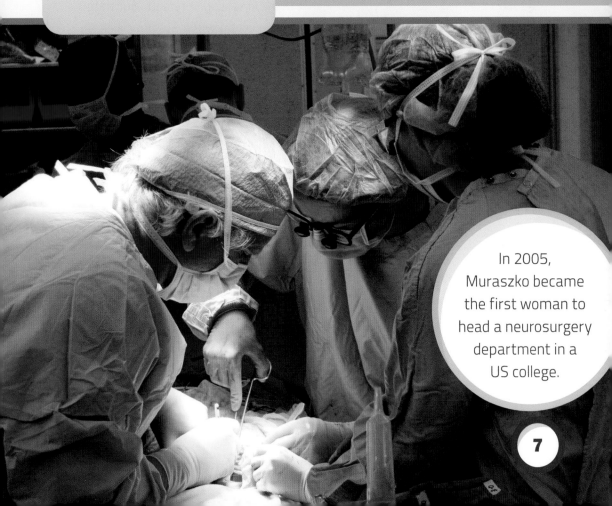

In 2005, Muraszko became the first woman to head a neurosurgery department in a US college.

Stephen Hawking: Searching for the Start of Time

When Stephen Hawking was 21 years old, doctors told him he had an incurable disease. The disease is called amyotrophic lateral sclerosis. It causes the nerves that control muscles to die. The doctors told Hawking he had less than three years to live.

Stephen Hawking in 2008.

Hawking was very sad. But then he noticed he wasn't getting sick as quickly as the doctors thought he would. He decided he would keep working as a theoretical physicist. This is a scientist who uses math to understand how things in nature and the universe work. Hawking wanted to find out as much as he could about where the universe came from.

Hawking lived for another 55 years. He became the most famous theoretical physicist in the world. He learned exciting new things about black holes, stars, and galaxies. The things he learned gave him important ideas about how the universe began.

Hawking made those discoveries even as his health got worse. Eventually, he could control only a

Hawking used math to study black holes and their effects on the universe.

few of his muscles. He used an electric wheelchair to get around. He also had a special computer that talked for him. He controlled what the computer said by moving a muscle in his cheek. Hawking died in 2018 at the age of 76.

10 million+

Copies sold of Stephen Hawking's most famous book

- It is called *A Brief History of Time.*
- It explains his ideas about the universe.
- Hawking also wrote several books for kids.

THREE CENTURIES APART

Hawking liked to tell people that he was born exactly 300 years after the death of Galileo. Galileo was also a famous scientist. He used math to prove that the earth travels around the sun. Galileo died in Italy on January 8, 1642. Hawking was born in England on January 8, 1942.

A BRIEF HISTORY OF TIME

FROM THE BIG BANG TO BLACK HOLES

STEPHEN W. HAWKING

INTRODUCTION BY CARL SAGAN

Hugh Herr: Building Bionic Legs

In 1982, Hugh Herr and a friend were caught in a blizzard on a mountain in New Hampshire. The two young men had been rock climbing. They spent three days and nights huddled together on the mountain, trying to stay warm. The temperature dropped as low as -20 degrees Fahrenheit (-29°C).

Herr and his friend survived that scary event. But by the time they were rescued, they had suffered severe frostbite. At the hospital, both of Herr's legs had to be amputated below the knee. The frostbite had caused the skin and tissue on his lower legs to die.

Herr was only 17 years old. Even at that young age, he was one of the most famous mountain climbers in the United States. Most people now thought Herr would never climb

1982
Year when Hugh Herr was fitted with his first prosthetic legs

- They were heavy, stiff, and made of plastic.
- Today, Herr uses different bionic legs for different activities.
- He uses some legs for walking and others for swimming. He has special legs he uses just for rock climbing.

Herr in 2014 using the bionic legs he invented.

again. He proved them wrong. He climbed mountains again. And he did it on artificial legs he invented himself.

After he lost his legs, Herr became a biomechanical engineer. This is someone who uses science and technology to make things that can be used in the human body. Herr designs and builds bionic arms and legs. They are made of a lightweight metal. They have tiny computers in them that run on batteries. They are specially designed so they feel and move like regular arms and legs.

Herr's bionic devices have changed many lives. They make it possible for people without an arm or a leg to do activities—like running, climbing, and dancing—they couldn't do otherwise.

Wanda Diaz Merced: Listening to the Stars

When Wanda Diaz Merced was growing up in Puerto Rico in the 1980s, she wanted to be an astronaut. She pretended her sister's bed was a spaceship. She and her sister would imagine traveling to different galaxies.

At college, Merced decided to become an astrophysicist. This is a scientist who studies planets, stars, and other objects in space. But when Merced was in her twenties, she began to lose her eyesight due to an illness. By 29, she was completely blind.

Merced thought her dream of becoming an astrophysicist had ended. But then she learned about sonification. This is a way of turning data—collections of measurements and other facts—into sound.

Here's how it works: Merced gathers data from space, such as how long explosions last on huge stars known as supernovas. She uses a computer to translate that data into sounds. Merced then listens to the sounds over and over again. By listening very carefully, she can sometimes pick out unusual patterns in the sounds. Those patterns help her and other scientists learn new things about the supernovas.

Today, Merced works as an astrophysicist in South Africa. She travels around the world to talk with kids who want to be scientists. She tells them not to give up on their dreams.

Wanda Diaz Merced uses her laptop to demonstrate sonification at a 2016 conference.

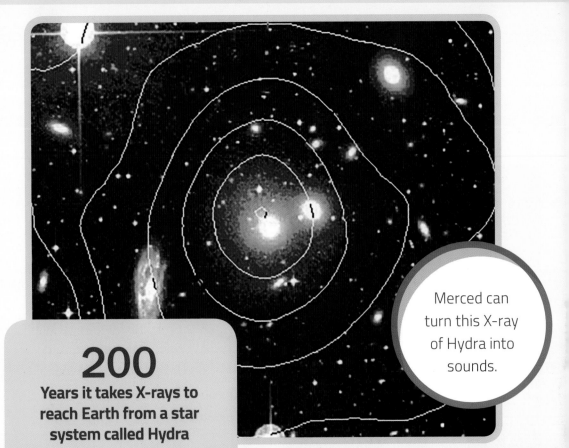

Merced can turn this X-ray of Hydra into sounds.

200

Years it takes X-rays to reach Earth from a star system called Hydra

- Merced has turned the X-ray data into sounds.
- A German composer used the sounds to create nine songs.
- Those songs are on a music album called *X-Ray Hydra*.

X-RAY HYDRA
VOLKMAR STUDTRUCKER
FEAT. GERHARD SONNLEIT & HANS-PETER ALBRECHT

BACK ON EARTH

Sonification is used to study things on earth as well as in outer space. It's used a lot by doctors. An example is a heart monitor machine. It measures how fast a person's heart is beating. The measurements are turned into beeping sounds. The beeps help doctors make sure the heart is working properly.

6

Solomon Lefschetz: Using Math to Solve Problems

Solomon Lefschetz with chalk in his wooden right hand.

it would be easier to get a job. An engineer is someone who uses science and technology to design or build things.

When he was 19 years old, Lefschetz went to the United States. He found a job working as an engineer for an electric company in Pittsburgh,

29
Years Solomon Lefschetz taught math at Princeton University in New Jersey

- When he taught, he wore wooden hands covered with black gloves.
- He would wedge a piece of chalk between the wooden fingers.
- He used the chalk to write math equations on a blackboard.

Solomon Lefschetz was born in Russia in 1884. When he was a baby, his family moved to France. That's where he went to school. His favorite subject was math. He was very good at it. But after he left school, Lefschetz decided to become an engineer instead of a mathematician. He thought

14

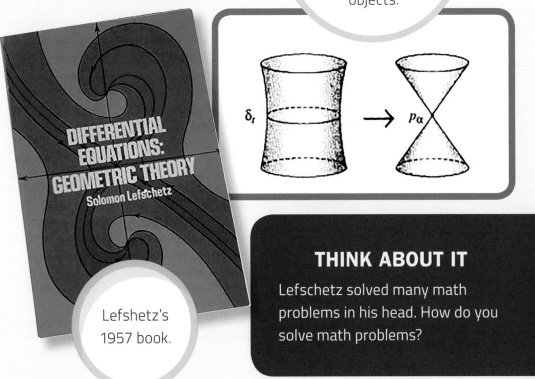

Lefschetz studied the distance between points on multi-dimensional objects.

Lefshetz's 1957 book.

THINK ABOUT IT

Lefschetz solved many math problems in his head. How do you solve math problems?

Pennsylvania. One day, there was an explosion in his laboratory. Both his hands were blown off.

It took Lefschetz many months to recover from the injuries. He was sad for a long time. He thought his career as an engineer was over. But then he remembered how much he enjoyed doing math. He decided to go back to school to become a mathematician.

Lefschetz became one of the most famous mathematicians in the world. He helped solve many mathematical problems. He also used math to make things work better. During World War II, for example, he worked closely with the US Navy. Using math, he showed the navy how to build ships that floated more safely in the sea.

James Lupski: Tracking Down Genetic Clues

James Lupski in 2012.

Lupski missed the first two years of high school. He stayed home because he had to have 10 operations on his feet and ankles. He read a lot of books on science and medicine while he was at home. He wanted to understand his disease.

He learned that Charcot-Marie-Tooth is an inherited disease. It is passed through genes from parents to children. Genes are tiny structures inside every cell in the human body. They carry information that helps make you who you are and what you look like. Genes determine the color of your eyes, for example, or how you laugh. Some genes are also linked to diseases.

James Lupski was born in New York in 1957 with Charcot-Marie-Tooth disease. It is a rare disease that damages the nerves in the arms and legs. Lupski didn't know he had the disease until he was 15 years old. That's when he started having trouble walking. His damaged nerves had caused his muscles to weaken. He also began to lose feeling in his hands and feet.

Lupski grew up to become a doctor and a scientist. He studies inherited diseases. He has made many important discoveries about them. He has even found out which specific genes cause Charcot-Marie-Tooth disease. Those findings may one day lead to a treatment.

30

Number of genes linked to Charcot-Marie-Tooth disease

- James Lupski discovered the first one in 1991.
- He discovered many of the other ones, too.
- Different genes are linked to different types of the disease.

NOTHING TO DO WITH TEETH

Charcot-Marie-Tooth disease is named after the three scientists who first identified the disease in 1886. One of those scientists was an Englishman called Howard Henry Tooth.

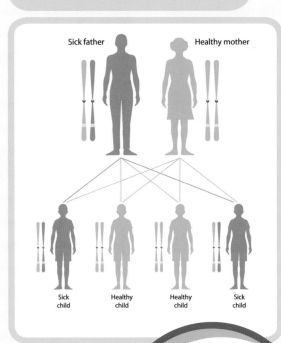

Sick father   Healthy mother

Sick child   Healthy child   Healthy child   Sick child

Charcot

Marie

Tooth

Inherited diseases are passed through genes from parents to their children.

Temple Grandin: Understanding Animals

Temple Grandin has autism spectrum disorder. It makes her see, hear, and feel the world differently than other people. For example, she sees the world in pictures rather than words. She also finds it

100+
Number of scientific papers Temple Grandin has published

- She has done research on how stress affects animals.
- Grandin says animals should not be treated like things.
- She wants all animals to have a good life.

Temple Grandin in 2010.

really difficult to understand other people's feelings. She can't tell if they are happy or sad.

Grandin was born in 1947. At that time, people didn't understand autism. She was bullied in school for being different. But not everyone was mean to her. She had friends who shared her interest in horses, electronics, and model rockets.

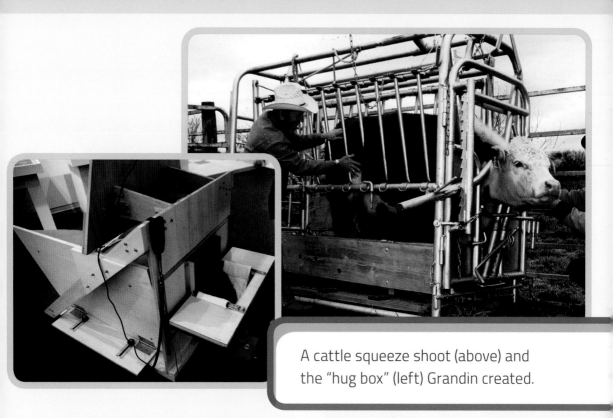

A cattle squeeze shoot (above) and the "hug box" (left) Grandin created.

She also had a science teacher who encouraged her to become a scientist.

When Grandin was 15, she visited a ranch in Arizona. She saw that cattle and horses calmed down when put in a squeeze chute. That's a special cage that holds animals while a veterinarian examines them. Grandin wanted to build a squeeze chute for herself. She thought it could help her feel calmer, too.

With help from her science teacher, Grandin built the first "hug box" for people with autism. Here's how it works: When you get inside the box, you pull a lever. It makes the sides of the box gently squeeze against you. The squeezing feels like a hug. The hug box has helped many people with autism feel less anxious.

Grandin's visit to the ranch changed her life. She became an animal scientist. That's someone who studies how to take better care of animals raised on ranches and farms. Over the years, Grandin has shown ranchers and farmers many ways to be kinder to their animals.

Rafael San Miguel: Making Food Taste Better

however. At college, he studied food science. He learned about the chemicals and other things that give foods their taste and smell. He also learned about how those things change when foods are processed and stored. After college, San Miguel went to work at the National Aeronautics and Space Administration (NASA). His job was to help develop special foods that astronauts could eat when they are in space.

Today, San Miguel works as a flavor scientist for a big company. A flavor scientist is someone who figures out how natural and artificial flavors can make processed foods taste better. Flavor scientists have to be good at chemistry. They also have to have strong taste buds and a sharp sense of smell.

San Miguel believes that because he lost one sense — his hearing — his senses of taste and smell are especially good.

When he was growing up in Missouri in the 1970s, Rafael San Miguel wanted to be an astronaut and travel into space. But as he got older, he realized it was unlikely he would ever fly on a spaceship. Why? Because he wouldn't be able to talk with the Mission Control crew back on earth. San Miguel has been deaf since he was a few days old.

He still wanted to work for the space program,

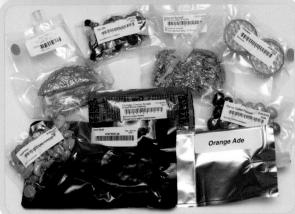

Food scientists testing flavors in a NASA lab.

Orange Ade

2012

Year when Rafael San Miguel was honored as a Champion of Change

- He received the award at the White House.
- President Barack Obama presented it to him.
- San Miguel got the award for inspiring kids to become scientists.

THINK ABOUT IT

Not everybody likes the same foods. But people can learn to like foods they once thought tasted terrible. Are there foods you like now that you didn't used to like?

Richard Mankin: Trapping Insects with Sounds

Richard Mankin examines insect sounds collected in the field.

hasn't let it keep him from doing his science outdoors, either.

Mankin is an entomologist. This is a scientist who studies insects. On many days, you can find him in fields or forests, searching for insects. When Mankin finds the insects, he listens to them. He has helped to develop a special piece of listening equipment. It can hear the sounds insects make while munching on their food or crawling around in the soil. When insects chomp on wood, for example, they make the wood vibrate—like a violin string.

Mankin uses his equipment to find hidden infestations of insects. An infestation is a large number of insects in a place where they are not wanted. Insect infestations often cause damage. For example, they can destroy crops that people use for food.

Richard Mankin was born in 1948 with a rare muscle disease. He has some muscles missing from his legs. To stand, he wears metal leg braces. To walk, he uses crutches. Getting around is difficult for Mankin. But he hasn't let that keep him from following his childhood dream of becoming a scientist. He

Mankin listening for insect infestation.

Mankin has also invented sound devices that trap insect pests, like mosquitoes, midges, cockroaches, and fruit flies.

5
Years it takes the Asian citrus psyllid to kill an orange tree

- This tiny insect eats the leaves of orange trees.
- While eating, it puts poison into the trees.
- Richard Mankin is trying to use sound to keep these insects away from orange trees.

WHAT ENTOMOLOGISTS DO

Agricultural entomologists (like Mankin) help farmers protect their crops from insects. Medical entomologists keep insects from spreading disease. Veterinary entomologists protect animals from insects. Taxonomic entomologists search for new insects, especially in the world's tropical rainforests. Structural entomologists look for ways to keep insects out of buildings.

Farida Bedwei: Designing Computer Programs

Farida Bedwei was born in the African country of Nigeria in 1979. An illness at birth caused her to develop cerebral palsy (CP). This is a condition that affects the body's muscles. Bedwei's leg muscles are weak. She uses crutches when walking. Her mouth muscles are also weak. She talks a bit more slowly than other people.

When Bedwei was nine years old, she and her family moved to Ghana, which is also in Africa. It was there that she became really interested in computers. She enjoyed using computers to solve problems and to create things.

Bedwei skipped high school. Instead, she went to a special school to learn about computers. At 15, she was the youngest person in the school. Later, she went to a university in Great Britain to learn even more about computers.

Today, Bedwei is one of the most successful software engineers in Africa. A software engineer is a computer scientist who designs programs (software) for computers. The programs tell computers to do certain kinds of things.

Bedwei owns and runs her own software company. Her company is especially well known for creating

Farida Bedwei in 2018.

software that helps Africans who are trying to start small businesses. Bedwei is also famous in Africa for speaking and writing about what it's like to have a disability. She wants people with disabilities to be treated just like everyone else.

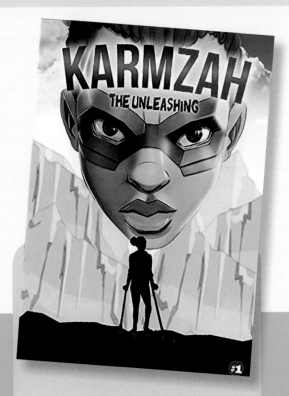

THE SHRINKING COMPUTER

The first electronic computers were built in the 1940s. They were huge. Each was the size of an entire room. Computers today are much smaller. Some are even smaller than a grain of sand.

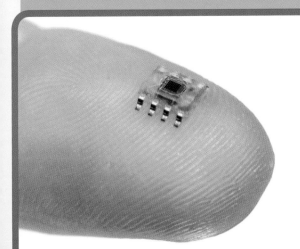

2018
Year when Farida Bedwei published a comic book called *Karmzah: The Unleashing*

- Karmzah is a superhero with cerebral palsy.
- Her crutches give her the power to run, jump, flip, fly, and fight.
- Karmzah fights bad guys, just like other superheroes.

Leo Lesquereux: Uncovering the Secrets of Ancient Bogs

Leo Lesquereux was born in Switzerland in 1806. His family lived in a small mountain village. Lesquereux spent much of his boyhood outdoors. That's where he was happiest. He especially liked going to a nearby peat bog. A peat bog is a place where dead plants— often mosses—have decayed over millions of years. Its ground is wet and spongy.

Lesquereux didn't just play in the peat bog. He studied it. He wanted to know exactly when and how the bog was formed. When Lesquereux was a boy, peat was very important to people in Switzerland. They cut it into bricks. Then they burned the bricks in their fireplaces to heat their homes.

Lesquereux became a teacher when he grew up. But he had to quit that job when he was 26 years old. He got sick. The illness caused him to lose his hearing. Lesquereux worried about getting another job. Then an American scientist invited him to come to the United States to study plants. Lesquereux decided to go. He eventually settled in Columbus, Ohio.

Within a few years, Lesquereux became one of the world's first—

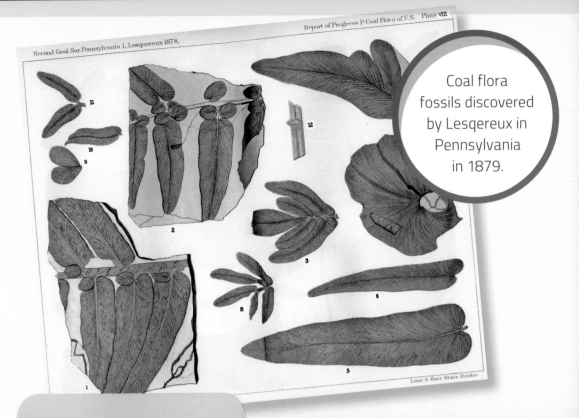

Second Geol. Sur. Pennsylvania. L. Lesquereux 1878,

Lane S. Hart. State Printer.

Coal flora fossils discovered by Lesqereux in Pennsylvania in 1879.

300 million
Years ago when coal was formed

- The earth had lots of steamy swamps filled with peat.
- Over time, rocks pressed against the peat. That squeezed the water out and turned the peat to coal.
- Lesquereux was the first person to link peat with coal.

THINK ABOUT IT

What is your favorite place to go outdoors? What plants or animals in that place would you like to learn more about?

and most famous—paleobotanists. Those are scientists who study plant fossils in places like bogs. His discoveries led to a better understanding of how the earth's surface has changed over time.

27

Learn More: The Individuals with Disabilities Education Act

In 1975, the United States Congress passed a special law to help children with disabilities. Today that law is known as the Individuals with Disabilities Education Act, or IDEA.

The idea behind IDEA is to make sure that children with disabilities get a free public education. In most cases, that means making sure they can go to the same schools as kids who aren't disabled.

Children with disabilities sometimes need extra help in school. Because of their disability, they may need help getting around inside the school. Or they might need a longer time to take a test. The Individuals with Disabilities Education Act makes sure those kids get that extra help.

The law covers children with most kinds of disabilities, including deafness, blindness, autism spectrum disorder, and paralysis. In some cases, it also covers children who have learning disabilities or who have trouble concentrating in class.

Each year, almost six million American children receive services under the Individuals with Disabilities Education Act. It's a law that has made many people's lives better.

Glossary

black hole
An area in space with gravity so strong that light can't escape. Scientists believe black holes are created when a huge star collapses.

fossil
The remains (or impressions) of plants or animals that lived long ago.

galaxy
Millions or billions of stars and planets that are held together by gravity.

incurable
Impossible to cure.

ocean reef
A long, raised line of rock, sand, and coral on the ocean floor.

spine
The row of bones down a person's back.

superhero
A made-up character in a book, comic book, or movie who has extraordinary or superhuman powers. A superhero can be a man or a woman—or a child.

surgery
A medical procedure in which a person's body is cut open.

veterinarian
A doctor who gives medical care and treatment to animals.

X-rays
A type of high-energy radiation. Many objects in space give off X-rays, including black holes and supernovas.

Read More

Bedwei, Farida. *Karmzah: The Unleashing.* Accra, Ghana, India: Leti Arts, 2019.

Edwards, Chris. *All About Stephen Hawking.* Indianapolis, IN: Blue River Press, 2018.

Mosca, Julia Finley. *The Girl Who Thought in Pictures: The Story of Dr. Temple Grandin.* Seattle, WA: The Innovation Press, 2017.

Visit 12StoryLibrary.com

Scan the code or use your school's login at **12StoryLibrary.com** for recent updates about this topic and a full digital version of this book. Enjoy free access to:

- Digital ebook
- Breaking news updates
- Live content feeds
- Videos, interactive maps, and graphics
- Additional web resources

Note to educators: Visit 12StoryLibrary.com/register to sign up for free premium website access. Enjoy live content plus a full digital version of every 12-Story Library book you own for every student at your school.

Index

About the Author

Susan Perry lives in Virginia with her
family. She writes about science and
health for children and grown-ups.
She wants to thank her grandson,
Colin, for all his help.

**READ MORE FROM
12-STORY LIBRARY**

Every 12-Story Library Book
is available in many fomats.
For more information, visit
12StoryLibrary.com